SAILS

Fernhurst Books

SAILS
Choice, trim and improvement

John Heyes

photographs by Tim Hore

First published 1987 by
Fernhurst Books, 53 High Street, Steyning, W. Sussex

ISBN 0 906754 29 1

Acknowledgements
The publishers would like to thank all those who sailed in the photo sessions: Steve
Drakeford and Gordon Kingston (505); Glyn Charles, Max Walker and Andy
Beadsworth (Norman Cunningham's Soling); Rob McMillan (Finn).
 The cover photograph is by Kos, and the cover design is by Behram Kapadia.

All the photographs in this book are by Tim Hore, with the following exceptions:
page 24 (right): Hamo Thorneycroft Marine Photography; page 41: Kos; page 8:
Francois Richard; pages 27, 30 and 46: Yachting Photographics.

Design by PanTek, Maidstone
Composition by A & G Phototypesetters, Knaphill
Printed and bound in Great Britain by Ebenezer Baylis & Son Ltd, Worcester.

Contents

1 How sails work   7
2 Sailmaking   15
3 Planning your campaign   28
4 Sail setting   36
5 Spinnakers   47
6 Fault finder   54
7 Care and repair   60

1   How sails work

There are many explanations of how a sail works, but most of them seem to assume the reader has a degree in aerodynamics. Since this is a big assumption, we will use a fairly simple concept: that of the sail as an 'air deflector'.

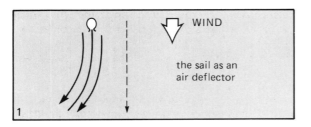

the sail as an air deflector

WIND

In the absence of a sail or other obstacle the wind will usually blow in a straight line (fig. 1). But put a sail in the path of the wind and the airflow is deflected. Some force is obviously at work on the air particles, directing them to the right, and since action and reaction are always equal and opposite the air particles will pull the sail to the left.

Another theory assumes that the air flowing around the lee side of the sail has to travel further than the air on the windward side. This reduces the pressure on the lee side, and the sail is 'sucked' to leeward.

Whichever theory you prefer, the effect is the same: because the sail is made of cloth it will move until the forces on it are acting at right-angles to its surface. Since the sail is curved the forces at each point will act in slightly different directions (fig. 2). For clarity, however, they can be

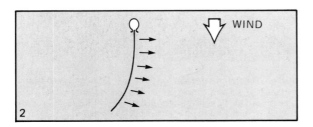

WIND

represented by one large vector arrow (fig. 3). This is the overall (or total) force on the sail: force F.

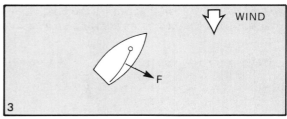

WIND

F can be split into two parts: the part which does useful work thrusting the boat forward (T), and the part which simply pushes the boat sideways (H). H is resisted by the keel or centreboard, with the result that the boat tends to heel over.

The larger the curve (or belly) in the sail, the greater the deflection of the air particles and the greater the power that is developed. F increases and so does T, so the boat will go faster.

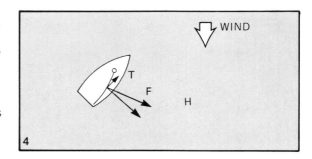

WIND

Unfortunately, H also increases, and there comes a point when the boat will capsize. That is why the mast is bent to flatten the sails and reduce their power in strong winds.

As the boat bears away and the mainsheet is eased (fig. 5) F swings round and points in a more useful direction. In other words, H is reduced and T is increased, so the boat goes forwards faster and with less heel.

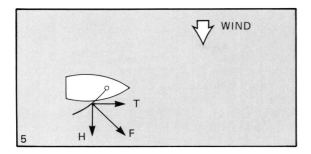

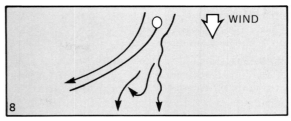

As the boat bears away still more (fig. 6) the wind can no longer flow over the sail and the 'air deflector' effect is lost. It is simply the force of the air hitting the sail that pushes the boat along on a run, and progress is slower than on a beat or a reach.

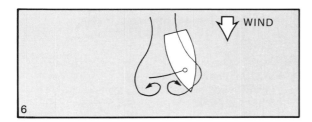

Break point

If you have ever looked out of an aircraft window as the plane flies through cloud, you may have seen the attached flow over the wing break into turbulent eddies near the trailing edge. The same happens on the leeward side of a sail, beginning at the 'break point' (fig. 7).

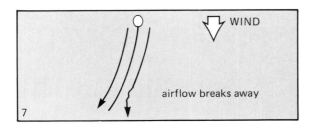

Although some separation of flow is inevitable towards the leech of the sail, the objective is to keep this to a minimum and keep the flow attached for as long as possible. That is one reason why oversheeting a sail is so deadly: the deflection expected of the air is too great, the flow breaks away too early, and drive is lost (fig. 8).

The role of the jib

The jib operates as an air deflector in the same way as the mainsail, but it also performs a vital role in training the airflow across the leeward side of the main. The presence of the jib increases the pressure around the lee side of the mast, which in turn causes a decrease in the apparent wind speed at this point. The slowing of airflow at the luff has two effects:
- The resistance to stall is increased, (because susceptibility to stall is directly related to windspeed).
- The lower apparent windspeed alters the direction of the force on the front of the mainsail. As a result the jib effectively puts the main into a 'header'. This is one reason why the mainsail is sheeted closer to the centreline than the jib, and it makes possible a slightly higher angle of attack and greater thrust.

Above: A Finn in classic upwind trim. The draft on a una rig is well aft to keep the flow attached as far back as possible, and this results in large sideways forces. To counteract this the boom must be sheeted well down to leeward.

Slot effect

As the jib is sheeted in closer to the main, the velocity of flow through the slot is diminished, until it matches the velocity on the windward side of the main. At this point the slot is acting at maximum efficiency. Thereafter, as the jib is brought in closer to the main, the flow through the slot drops further; the leeside pressure builds up and causes the main to backwind.

Contrary to popular theory, the jib does not serve to speed up flow through the slot, but in fact slows it. Both main and jib work by deflecting the airflow but the slot effect greatly improves the efficiency of the jib, while slightly lowering that of the main. In combination, the thrust of main and jib is greater than that of the two sails working separately. This does however make trimming the sails a harder task, as not only does each sail have to be sheeted to do its own job properly; it also has to be so positioned that it maximises the efficiency of the other.

Una-rigs

The Laser, Finn and O.K. sails work in much the same way as other mainsails, but with one important difference. Normally the break point – the position on the leeward side where the attached flow breaks away from the sail and becomes turbulent flow – coincides with the maximum draft position. Aft of this it becomes increasingly difficult to keep the flow attached to the sail, and it breaks away and follows the tangent of that part of the curve. On a una-rig boat the break point occurs sooner, owing to the absence of a jib to train the flow around the leeward side. To combat this problem the maximum depth is set a little further aft, in an attempt to keep the flow attached for longer; more importantly the sail is set at a greater angle to the centreline. With the traveller well down to leeward, the overall force on the sail (F) swings forward and the thrust force (T) is increased to an efficient level.

SOME DEFINITIONS

Before discussing sail shapes, it is useful to become familiar with a little terminology.

Aspect ratio

The aspect ratio describes the basic proportions of a sail. The narrower the sail, the higher the aspect ratio. In general, a high-aspect sail provides better upwind performance, as it provides the highest lift and lowest drag. The optimum aspect ratio for beating would have a luff length of three times the foot length, whereas for reaching a much lower-aspect sail is faster. However, the high-aspect rig produces greater heeling forces, as the centre of effort is positioned higher in the sail.

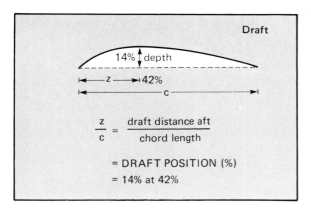

$$\frac{z}{c} = \frac{\text{draft distance aft}}{\text{chord length}}$$

= DRAFT POSITION (%)

= 14% at 42%

Above: The draft stripes on this Soling enable the draft to be assessed on the water, and from photographs.

Depth

Sail depth is defined as the ratio of the depth of curvature to the chord length. The chord is the line from the leech to the luff. Described in percentage terms, the depth of the sail in the diagram is 14% of the total chord length.

Above: Attaching draft stripes. Take a tuck in the sail so it lies flat. Then stick on the stripes parallel to the waterline at the quarter heights.

Draft

The position of greatest depth in the sail, at a particular height, is known as the 'draft position', and is again described in percentage terms of total chord length. The draft in the diagram is located at 42% of the chord length, measured aft from the mast. So a complete description of the sail shape is 14% depth at 42% aft'.

Depth and draft are commonly measured by the sailmaker at the quarter, half and three-quarter heights of the sail. Trim stripes should be marked on the sail at these heights to give the eye a greater appreciation of draft and to serve as a reference when draft is measured from photographs. Trim stripes should be placed on the sail parallel to the waterline, so that the section through the sail is horizontal. Fast sails are generally deeper in the head than in the foot.

Angle of attack

The angle of attack is a measure of the roundness of the luff. A small angle of attack gives a fine entry and good pointing ability. A more rounded entry is less prone to stall, however, and provides more power in waves but results in a lower pointing angle. It is harder to sail with a fine-entried sail, as the difference between luffing and stalling is small; a sail with a more rounded entry is more forgiving as it allows a wider range of headings before the sail luffs or stalls.

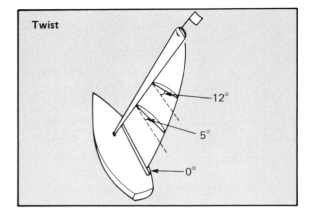

Left: Small angle of attack (a); large angle of attack (b).
Below left and right: To compare the twist in sails take photographs straight down the boom. Draw a line from the head to the clew (1). Then draw a second line at right angles, to the point of maximum twist (2). Express 2 as a percentage of 1, to give the degree of twist.

Above: To record the draft and depth of your sails as shown here, first log the windspeed and wave heights. Then take photographs of the sails from below, using print film. From the prints, measure the depth and draft as a percentage of chord length (there is a proprietary scale available to make this job easier).

Twist

Twist is defined as the variation in chord angle up the sail. It is either described in degrees or, when measuring from photographs, in percentages. The correct amount of twist means that the whole sail will luff at the same time. Much has been written about vertical wind gradients and wind shear demanding more twist on starboard tack than on port, depending on which hemisphere you are in! In reality, these effects are usually overestimated; indeed they are sometimes reversed by temperature inversion effects and general air turbulence. The greatest windspeed gradient occurs within a frictional layer of a few wave heights, and within the range of a dinghy mast there may be a 5% variation.

CLOTH

Sailcloth is described in terms of its weight, finish and stretch characteristics.

Cloth weight

Cloth weight is either measured in US oz/square yard, g/m^2 or occasionally UK oz/square yard, so be careful to check the measure specified in the class rules. The weights of many cloths do not coincide exactly with the weights printed on the labels, as they are product names rather than actual weights. It is worth bearing this point in mind when selecting sail material for a class which restricts the cloth that can be used. '6.0 oz Dacron', may in fact weight 5.75 oz, and this may not qualify under the class rules.

Cloth stretch

Cloth stretch plays a vital part in determining the shape of a sail. The sailmaker's main aim is to build a sail which will set in its designed shape in the widest possible range of conditions. If he selects a cloth which is too stretchy, the shape may be perfect in 6 knots of breeze, but a disaster in 15 knots.

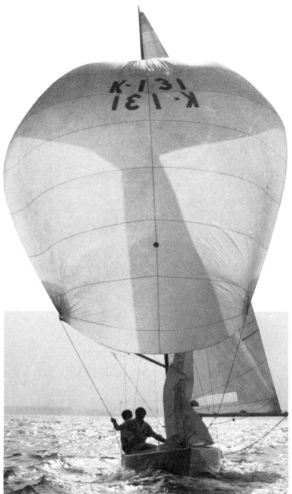

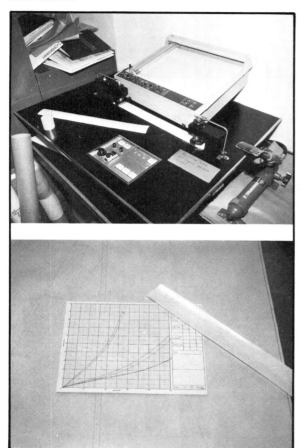

Above: This machine tests the stretch characteristics of cloth in three directions, to ensure the fabric matches the design specifications for the sail. A graph is printed out showing the distortion under load in each stretch direction. A second sample of cloth is then fluttered to simulate use, and the test repeated (giving pairs of lines on the graph).

Cloth is made from threads which run in two directions: the 'warp' threads which run in the long axis of the cloth, and the 'fill' or 'weft' threads which run across the long axis. The amount of stretch in these two directions is mainly governed by the size of the threads and their density of packing, but the warp commonly stretches less. A weaver may set up a warp of 5000 to 10 000 metres, across which the fill threads are woven one at a time and tightly pounded into place. This causes the fill threads to become 'crimped' as they pass alternately under and over the warp. When placed under load, the crimped yarns of the weft straighten out, resulting in much greater stretch in this direction than in the straight warp threads.

The ratio of fill to warp stretch can however be adjusted by altering the relative sizes of the yarns in each direction. For example, the sail designer can choose different threads to match the loads in a cross-cut sail, where the maximum loading is on the leech and is therefore carried by the fill threads. As we have already seen, the continuous warp threads are naturally stronger than the crimped fill fibres. In order for the fill to be the stronger orientation, the fibres must necessarily be larger or more numerous than the warp fibres to withstand the higher loading of the leech.

Bias stretch

The greatest stretch occurs at 45 degrees to the fill and warp, and this is known as the bias direction. Bias stretch is a result of the weave construction. Under load the threads pivot at their intersection points and the rectangular areas between the fibres are pulled into parallelograms. In order to reduce bias stretch, the cloth manufacturer applies a resin dressing to the weave, which impregnates the fibres and glues the threads into position, so reducing the amount of stretch. The stiffness of a cloth is partly determined by how much resin is applied during the finishing process. There are often several finishes available for a particular cloth weight, ranging from soft, via medium firm, to yarn tempered which is the stiffest. The yarn tempered finish is produced by applying considerable resin to the weave and then passing it through heated rollers. Small lines ('crazing') will appear in the sail with use, as the stiff finish cracks where it has been folded, or where the genoa clew hits the mast during tacking.

Below: The large mast bend of the Finn (left) demands a high bias stretch. The 505 mast (right) bends less, so the main can be made of stiffer cloth (yarn tempered or Mylar).

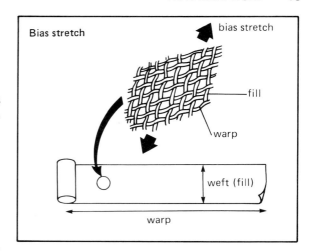

Above: Stretching the cloth in the bias direction pulls the fibres out of square. A resin dressing applied to the weave prevents this happening.

WHICH CLOTH?

The next area to consider is why a sail designer selects a certain fabric for a particular sail. We have already seen that sails of different aspect ratio have different load distributions and hence require different fabrics.

Headsails

As the jib is primarily an up-wind sail, it has to operate in conditions of high apparent wind speed. Furthermore it does not have the benefit of a sail placed in front (as in the case of the mainsail), to slow and train the airflow. For these reasons it is desirable to have a jib which will maintain its shape through the wind range, so the majority of racing classes use jibs or genoas built from a stiff yarn tempered cloth. Another reason for this is to keep to a minimum the extra fullness caused by the forestay sagging to leeward in a breeze.

Mainsails

Mainsails are commonly built from a fairly firm cloth, which has fill threads strong enough to withstand leech loading, but also has sufficient bias stretch at the luff to match the likely range of mast bend. The panel orientation in a cross-cut sail puts the fill threads parallel to the leech and the bias direction parallel to the luff. In the case of a jib, a certain amount of bias stretch is necessary at the luff to make the sail responsive to halyard tension. For a mainsail, bias stretch at the luff is even more important. From the photos you can compare the mast bend of a Finn with that of a 505, which explains why the Finn sailcloth has a high bias stretch. In order to flatten the Finn sail, considerable mast bend is employed. If the bias stretch did not match the range of mast bend, it would be impossible to flatten the sail

and large creases would run from clew to luff. A 505 has a much smaller range of controlled mast bend, and can use a stiffer, less stretchy yarn tempered cloth.

In short, a large part of the sail designers' job is to choose a cloth with the correct stretch characteristics to match the mast bend, aspect ratio and sail shape he wishes to create.

Laminated sailcloths

Mylar* is a trade name for a polyester film which is commonly used for laminated fabrics, in the same way that the name Dacron* is used for woven polyester cloth. Chemically the two are the same. Dacron is extruded as fine filaments which are then spun into thread. Mylar is also extruded, but in long thin sheets which gives the material its uniform directional stretch characteristics. This is the reason Mylar scores over woven fabrics: it eliminates bias stretch. In practice a single film of Mylar is brittle and tears easily. For this reason, sailcloth Mylar consists of a layer of Mylar film bonded onto a woven Dacron substrate. The woven element improves the material's tear strength and flexibility, while the performance of the whole fabric depends upon the strength of the bonding agent. When Mylar first came out the adhesive was the weak link; this often resulted in delamination. Over the years much has been learnt about bonding techniques and Mylar failure is now a thing of the past.

Applications for Mylar

The benefits of reduced weight and stretch and increased durability make Mylar the ideal material for headsails. For mainsails, the weight saving advantage is still relevant, and so too is the reduced stretch factor in the leech. However, with a mainsail made of laminated fabric it is often difficult to remove fullness by bending the mast as the breeze gets up, because there is so little bias stretch. For this reason Mylar mainsails are only effective in those one-design boats which would otherwise use a yarn tempered cloth, such as the 505, which has a small, controlled degree of mast bend. For other classes, laminated sails would only fit a specific mast bend and would have only a very small wind range.

*Mylar and Dacron are Dupont registered trademarks

2 Sailmaking

While it is not necessary to know how to build sails to use them, it is useful to have an idea how they are put together when discussing your requirements with the sailmaker. The three shaping elements in a sail are the luff curve, broadseam and cloth stretch.

Luff curve

Before the days of panel shaping, curving the luff was the only method of putting shape into a sail. If a curve is cut on the front of a sail which is then set on a straight mast, the extra cloth forces shape into the sail. Relying on luff curve alone gives the sail a very unsatisfactory draft forward shape, however, and today the shape is created through a combination of luff curve and broadseam.

In the case of the jib, the luff curve becomes luff hollow, cut to match the envisaged luff sag.

Broadseam

The broadseam is simply the curved edge of the cloth panel, which when joined to the straight edge of the adjacent panel forces camber into the sail. Once the sail is seamed up it assumes a three-dimensional shape and will not lie flat on the floor. The amount of broadseam is critical,

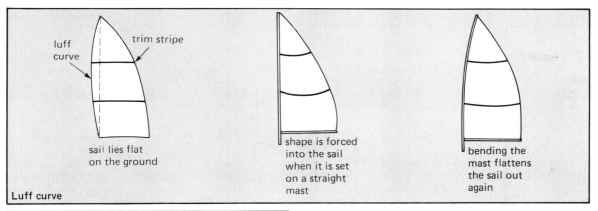

luff curve
trim stripe

sail lies flat on the ground

Luff curve

shape is forced into the sail when it is set on a straight mast

bending the mast flattens the sail out again

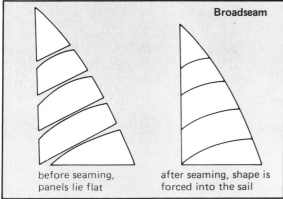

Broadseam

before seaming, panels lie flat

after seaming, shape is forced into the sail

and changes of only a few millimetres can make a dramatic difference to sail shape.

Small vertical darts or 'take-ups' in the foot panel curl the foot round up into a more powerful shape for offwind work.

Cloth stretch

Cloth stretch is an intrinsic part of a sail's design. For example, the most important element of a Finn sail is the cloth. As the wind builds, the bias stretch in the cloth makes the sail fuller in the leech, providing extra power.

MYLAR PATTERNS

Traditionally, one-design sails are built from full size Mylar patterns. Broadseams, battens, luff curve and leech positions are all marked on the Mylar sheet by raised tapes. The cloth is carefully rolled out across the pattern parallel to the marked 'roll' lines. It is important that the panels run at right angles to the leech so the strong fill threads take the high leech load.

Once the cloth is pinned in position, the broadseam is drawn onto the top edge of each panel by running a pencil along the lower raised edge of the tape on the pattern. The sail cutter then runs his scissors along the other side of the tape to trim off the excess cloth.

The bottom edge of the adjacent panel is left straight, so that when the two are seamed together shape is forced into the sail. Batten pockets are drawn on in a similar fashion. The ends of the battens serve to mark the leech position and should be arranged to accommodate the maximum girth measurements (across the sail) allowed by the class rules. The luff curve is usually drawn on as a series of marks on each panel which are later faired through once the panels have been sewn together.

Below and right: Making a sail. (1) The Mylar pattern has raised tapes to define the shapes of the broadseams, leech and luff, and the positions of the battens. (2) The curve of the broadseam is vital. Here the shape has been modified by adding a leech take-up. (3) The cloth is carefully pinned and then rolled out across the pattern at right angles to the leech.

1

2

3

Above: (4) The broadseam is transferred to the cloth by running a pencil down the lower edge of the raised tape. (5) The panel is cut by guiding the scissors along the upper edge of the tape. This gives a curved panel with a 15mm allowance for the seam.

Below: (6) Double-sided tape is stuck along the pencil line. (7) The straight (uncut) edge of the next panel is stuck down carefully along the pencil line. This puts curve into the sail.

Above and right: (8) The sail is held up to check that the join is smooth before seaming. (9) If all is well, the sail goes to the machinist to be stitched together. (10) The seam can be either a double row of zigzags (very strong) or a single row of triple step (which is light but not so strong). (11) The sail is returned to the floor for the second layout stage. The luff curve is drawn on using a batten to fair through the marks which have been transferred from the pattern. (12) Different luff curves can be selected to suit different mast bends.

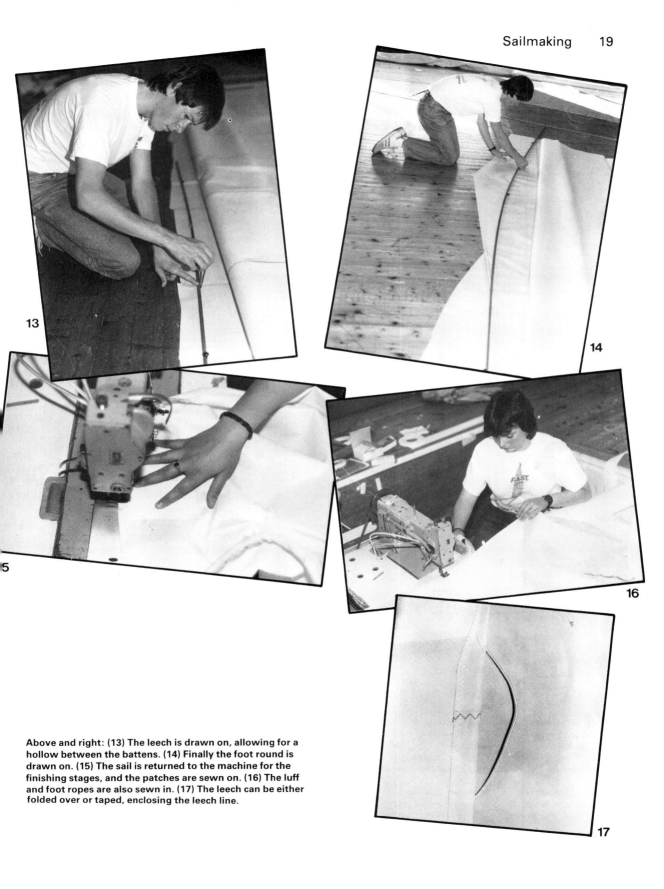

Above and right: (13) The leech is drawn on, allowing for a hollow between the battens. (14) Finally the foot round is drawn on. (15) The sail is returned to the machine for the finishing stages, and the patches are sewn on. (16) The luff and foot ropes are also sewn in. (17) The leech can be either folded over or taped, enclosing the leech line.

Recording the shape

The object of using a full-size pattern (rather than a list of offsets from a straight line) is to reproduce exactly the same sail shape every time. Drawn carefully, the broadseam should be accurate to within the width of a pencil line. The other great advantage of the full-size pattern is that it provides a record of several different luff curves.

It is worth ensuring that your sailmaker records any new design he may develop with you in this way, so that if it proves fast you can order the same shape again and be confident of getting it. Sail shape is very dependent upon the form of the broadseam: while there may be the same amount of broadseam in each panel, (measured as an offset from a straight line), the result can be very different, depending how the batten is faired through the points. Consequently sails which are hand-lofted from a series of offsets seldom come out the same twice.

Above: As an alternative to using the Mylar pattern, computer-designed sails are often cut direct from the computer program by a table plotter.

Computer cutting

An alternative method of cutting has been developed in the last few years by a few of the larger sail lofts, using computer-driven plotter tables. Computer cutting is a natural progression from computer designing or 'moulding' of sails, and removes the need for any Mylar patterns.

The sail is first created as a three-dimensional mould shape which is described numerically, but can also be viewed graphically on a VDU screen. The computer program then drapes cloth around the mould in any chosen fashion, with horizontal, vertical or radial panels, and calculates the broadseam necessary in each panel to achieve the designed shape. This information is then transferred directly to the table plotter which automatically cuts each panel of the sail. As the plotter arm moves up and down the table a suspended pen draws the seam line; a rotating high-speed cutting disc then trims a seam width outside the line. The cut panels are then ready for seaming. (An added advantage of describing sails numerically is that they can be transmitted around the world via telex or on floppy disc).

Whichever system of cutting sails your sailmaker uses, it is essential that it is accurate and reproduceable. The beauty of the computer design and cutting system is that a sail shape can be modified on the computer screen and then cut straight away without having to alter any templates. The computer-cut sail is fully described numerically, which allows shapes to be compared quantitatively. Depth, draft and twist measurements from photographs of the flying sail

can also be compared directly with the original design to check how closely the two correspond. A computer-cut sail is theoretically more accurate than one cut by hand as the variable human element is removed. However, in practice the smoothness of the sail will always depend on how well the panels are put together.

Gluing and seaming

Before seaming, the panels are carefully stuck together with double-sided sticky tape so there is no danger of the seam moving apart while it is being sewn. The straight bottom edge of one panel is glued down with double-sided tape along the pencil line drawn on the top edge of the adjacent panel. In fact the sticky tape contributes greatly to the strength of the seam, and is so strong that it is possible to stick several panels together and then hold them up before sewing to check that each seam is smooth. If there are any bumps, the seam can be pulled apart and restuck several times until the sailmaker is happy with the shape.

With yarn-tempered cloth, any wrinkle in the seam causes a major lump which stretches a long way into the panel, so any deviation from the fair curve of the broadseam line is magnified several times. The preliminary taping of the seams makes this much less likely during the actual operation of sewing the panels, as although the needle line may wander a little, the seam will not.

Stitching

The type of stitch used is dicated by the amount of loading placed on the seam, but for most one-design sails a triple-step seam is used. For higher-load applications, a double row of zig-zag stitches provides a slightly stronger seam.

The correct choice of thread weight, stitch tension and seam width is vital in order to achieve a smooth but strong seam. When seaming laminated fabrics, there is a tendency for the Mylar film to tear slightly around the needle holes as tension is applied to the seam. To prevent this 'seam creep', a sticky Dacron tape is applied to the seam on the shiny, Mylar side of the fabric before sewing. In the early days of Mylar sails, all seams were taped in this way, but with improvements in both fabrics and seaming techniques, seams are now only taped in high-load areas, mainly around the clew.

THE LAYOUT STAGE

Once all the panels are seamed together, with the batten pockets and windows sewn on, the sail returns to the floor to be layed out.

Luff curve

Matching the luff curve on the sail to the exact amount of mast bend in your rig is one of the most important factors in achieving correct sail shape. The sailmaker often has several luff curves marked on his pattern for the popular mast sections in use within the class. However, if you are using a new or different mast section, or if your rig set-up or crew weight demands that your mast bends differently from others, you will have to tell the sailmaker so that he may make the necessary modifications.

The luff curve is drawn onto the sail by pinning a batten along the marks from the Mylar pattern. The secret of obtaining a smooth and fair curve is

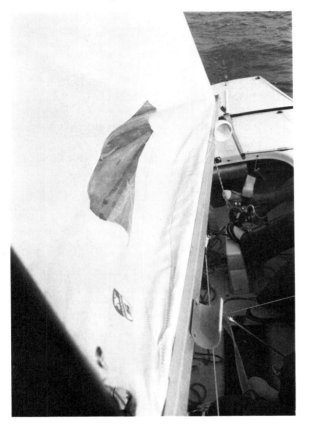

Above: The lensfoot is controlled by the outhaul. On the left the outhaul is off; on the right the outhaul is on.

a combination of a good pattern and an experienced sailmaker who can 'tweak' the batten to match the mast bend.

Trimming the leech

At layout, the position of the leech is already defined by the batten pocket ends and the head and clew. However, it is not simply a question of joining up the points with straight lines. In order to minimise leech flutter a certain amount of hollow is cut into the leech between each batten to keep the trailing edge under tension. The right amount of hollow is critical. Too much and the leech will not open easily, too little and it will flutter readily between battens. In the case of a jib, considerably more hollow is cut into the sail to prevent flutter, as a sail without battens is unable to support any degree of roach (roach is any area of sail behind a straight line from head to clew).

The leech of a mainsail may be finished off by folding over the cloth, or by trimming along the leech and sewing a folded tape over the edge. On a jib, folding the leech over tends to cause it to hook up; it is therefore normally finished with the lightest possible tape. The leech tape must be sewn on with a very loose tension, as if the stitch is at all tight, this too will cause the leech to hook up. For this reason some sailmakers simply hot knife the jib leech, although eventually the edge will begin to fray.

It is well worth having a leech line fitted to a large genoa as it can considerably extend the sail's life. All genoas will tend to flutter or vibrate on the leech as the breeze gets up, and if this is allowed to happen the cloth right on the edge of the sail will soon break down completely. Once this occurs the sail will begin to flutter in lower wind strengths and will soon become a major

problem. If a leech line is fitted, all that is needed is a little tension on the line to stop the fluttering completely.

Any genoa that is the size of a 505 or International 14 or larger will benefit from having a leech line fitted. A neat method of securing the tail of the line is inside a Velcro pocket. With this system the tab is adjustable; it does not catch on the shrouds and there are no loose ends to get wrapped around the rigging.

The foot

The foot is the last edge of the sail to be laid out. The jib foot is finished in a similar way to the leech, with a light tape. Usually, the sailmaker will opt for the maximum foot round allowed by the class rules.

Above: This radial patch is designed to hold the middle of the sail flat while allowing the leech to twist open.

Most racing mainsails these days are fitted with a shelf or lens foot, to ensure the sail takes up the correct horizontal camber directly above the boom. Without a shelf foot, there is an intermediate area above the boom where the sail is not setting in the best shape. The shelf is simply a lens-shaped panel of soft, stretchy cloth, cut along the bias direction, one edge of which is sewn onto the straight edge of the bottom panel of the sail and the other onto the bolt rope.

Patch engineering

Until quite recently, the reinforcement patch was an area of one-design sail development that had

been left relatively untouched, but a look around the dinghy park today will reveal a weird and wonderful assortment of patch styles.

The clew and head patch can be designed to fulfil one of several functions. The clew patch may be orientated towards the leech in an effort to support the lower leech and keep it tight. A similarly orientated patch at the head will prevent the top of the sail opening too early and falling off. Leech-orientated patches are most common on boats which are basically under-powered and require the leech to remain tight as long as possible, such as the 420 and 470.

By contrast, a radial patch can be shaped to hold the middle of the sail flat, for use in heavy airs, without supporting the leech. The leech is allowed to twist off, helping to depower the sail further.

Another type of clew patch has three long radial fingers, extending over the first batten. As well as supporting the leech, this patch helps control the inboard end of the batten, preventing

Above: The clew patches on these J24s have long vertical fingers to support the lower leech. Note also the pre-start window below the collision window in the genoa.

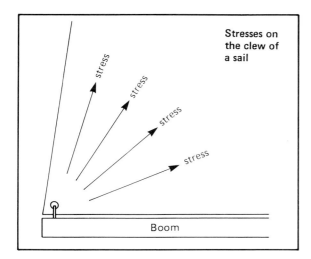

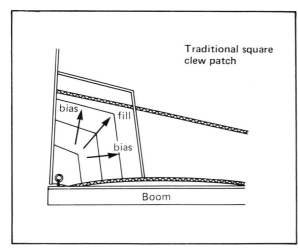

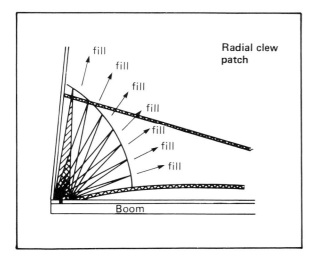

Above: This Finn sail is made from soft cloth, so it needs a small clew patch; a large patch would flatten the shape near the leech.

that all-too-familiar crease from the batten end to the clew. For boats required to have a reef point in the main (such as the J24) the clew cover patch should also span the reef reinforcement, otherwise creases will form in the relatively weaker area between the two patches.

Radial patches help to smooth the loading into a corner by spreading the load-bearing perimeter of the patch over a greater area. The radial segments should be cut on the strongest orientation of the cloth, (on the fill if cross-cut cloth is used) to reduce stretch to a minimum within the patch. Because of its greater efficiency, the radial patch can be built lighter than a conventional square patch; this not only reduces the all-up weight of the sail, but on a jib allows the sail to tack quicker and set more easily in light airs.

Large radial patches are not always the best answer. For a sail made of soft cloth a large, stiff patch may well flatten off a considerable area of the sail, destroying the designed shape. The sudden change in stretch characteristics where the patch finishes will also produce a bump and have a hinging effect with the load transferred to the softer cloth. The current vogue with some

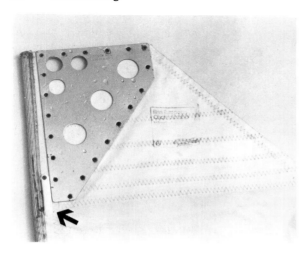

Above: Note the slug (arrowed) on this Finn headboard, which holds the headboard at the correct angle to the mast and tightens the leech.

look different. While some of these patches are effective, others alter the shape of the sail by suddenly changing the thread direction from warp to bias.

If engineered correctly and built in the right cloth, the reinforcement patch can make a major contribution to the overall performance of the sail and increase the sail's competitive lifespan. When discussing your sails with the loft ask the sailmaker to explain why he builds a particular patch; make sure it has been designed specifically for your type of sail, and is large enough for the job.

FINISHING

A number of refinements can be added to the basic sail structure which will often improve handling and performance.

Boltropes

To ease the operation of the shelf foot, have your

sailmakers is to build very complicated 'hi tech' clew and head patches, simply to make their sails

Above: A jib stuff luff. The luff tension is controlled by the jib cunningham (arrowed).

Above: A tape luff secured by poppers around the forestay. This is a common arrangement on keelboats.

sailmaker fit an 8 mm (5/16 in) diameter shock cord as the foot rope. The elastic is sewn in under tension so that once round the leeward mark the outhaul can be flicked off and the clew shoots inboard of its own accord. As long as a good clew slug is fitted (and the elastic is of sufficient diameter not to come out of the boom) shock cord can happily be used on Dragons, Solings and other keelboats. In una rigs, such as the Finn, O.K. and Europe, shock cord should be used for both luff and foot ropes.

Jib luff systems

The use of 'stuff luffs' with rod rigging and no jib halyard is becoming increasingly popular on high performance dinghies which demand high rig tension. If you are using a rod forestay, the jib luff tube must be made wide enough to slide over the end toggle fitting. At the head, a short webbing loop is sufficient to lash the sail to the jib strop. Luff tension can be applied by simply tying the tack down to the bow fitting or, if the class rules allow, it can be made adjustable with a cleat sewn onto the luff. The more common luff system is a stainless steel wire sewn into the luff tube with a swaged eye seized into the sail at both ends. Ask for 1 x 19 wire, which is stiffer and stretches less than the 7 x 7 variety.

Keelboat jibs such as those on the Star and Soling have no luff wire, just a heavy tape hanked onto the forestay. With this system it is easier to control draft position in the sail by altering luff tension with the jib halyard.

Handwork

The final stage in building a sail is to fit the hardware: headboard, press rings, leech line cleat and clew slug. The foot and luff ropes are tensioned to give them some elasticity; this makes the sail more responsive to halyard and outhaul control. Lastly, the numbers and telltales are attached and the sail is ready for action.

3 Planning your campaign

Assuming you are beginning a campaign in a new class, how do you go about choosing the fastest combination of sails and spars for your new boat? The best starting point is a visit to the Nationals or some other major championships, armed with a camera and a note book. Aim to compile a complete list of the equipment used by the top ten boats. Your list should include columns for the make of the hull, mast, mainsail, jib and spinnaker.

Check the boats in the dinghy park yourself to find exactly which mast sections and mainsails were used: don't rely on hearsay, which is invariably out of date. To do your homework properly, you need to find out not only which mast section was used but the length of the taper; whether the top section was pressed or internally or externally sleeved, and where. At one world championship, there were three versions of the same mast section in use within the top ten boats. Similarly with sails, you should note which sailmaker was used for each sail, and which design. Had the luff curve been modified, or had other changes been made from the original pattern?

Below left and right: Find out which are the top boats and take photos like these to get an idea of the amount of jib luff sag, mast rake and mast bend they use.

Rig shots

If you can manage to get on the water during your regatta visit, any photos of boats sailing upwind, from abeam and head on, will give you an indication of the current range of mast rake in the class, and how straight the masts are held sideways. Take as many photos as you can to help you make your choice of rig.

Many dinghy classes are not as one-design as you think, and permit quite a range of rig options, such as the use of diamonds on a Contender, a high or low jib box on a 505, single or double spreaders on an International 14.

When taking photos of the boats' layout, you should also note whether spinnaker bags or chutes are more popular and which system is easiest and fastest to use. In the case of the Fireball, the benefits stack up in favour of the bag system as the spinnaker is relatively small and quick to douse, and the boat remains a lot drier downwind without the chute.

However, on an International 14 the spinnaker is a lot larger and would take forever to stuff into a bag. Since the boats are undecked, there is little to gain from not using a chute.

The more regattas you can repeat this procedure for, the more consistent a picture you can build up of the performance of each item of equipment. For the less obvious details, such as the exact model name of a sail, you will have to ask the crew themselves. If this information is unforthcoming, a call to the supplier should provide all the answers you require.

Below: Hang up a jib like this to assess the shape.

Choosing a sailmaker

How far you pursue your research will depend on your own level of competition. If you are mainly involved in club racing, the standard version of the championship-winning rig will be fine. But if you are beginning an international or Olympic campaign, you may wish to start off by duplicating the current champions' equipment exactly.

By using the same rig as the fastest boats, you will have a 'boat speed benchmark' to work towards. When you feel that you are of a sufficient standard to develop new sails, your objective will be to surpass this benchmark, and you must choose a sailmaker who can help you do this. Apart from a proven reputation in the class and a good database of previous designs, he must:
- be active and interested in your class;
- be easily accessible to you;
- have something special to offer, such as high quality fabrics or 'hi-tech' constructions;
- be helpful and easy to work with.

The current market leader may not always be interested in updating his designs if they are already selling well. On the other hand, think carefully before working with a sail loft with no previous experience in your class, as the sailmaker may end up learning at your expense.

WHAT YOUR SAILMAKER NEEDS TO KNOW

For the majority of dinghy and keelboat sails the sailmakers' specification will be fairly complete, but he will still have several questions for you.

General sailing conditions

Some sailmakers produce different sail shapes for inland and coastal conditions. If most of your sailing is on flat inland waters, ask the sailmaker to ensure that your sails have a fine entry to the luff, for optimum pointing ability.

Mast section

The choice of mast affects the shape of the luff curve, and the use of an uncommon mast section may involve fitting non-standard bolt rope. Always advise the sailmaker which brand of spar you will be using. You should also advise how the mast is to be rigged:

- single or double spreaders;
- lower shrouds or diamonds;
- height of trapeze wires;
- whether a forward preventer or strut is to be used.

All these details decide the shape of the luff curve and help the sailmaker match the sail to the spar.

Crew weight

If the crew weight is particularly light or heavy you should tell the sailmaker. A big discrepancy from the norm will require the mast to be bent relatively more or less, and the luff curve will have to be altered to accommodate the difference.

Jib luff systems

Depending on the class rules, you may have a choice of jib luff system. If you are sailing a J24, you have a choice between the headfoil system or snap poppers. Using the poppers has the advantage of not needing a man on the foredeck to re-hoist the sail, but it is a lot slower than the headfoil when you come to change sails. The Dragon is one of the few keelboat classes which allow a zipper luff; this totally encloses the forestay and allows for rapid sail changes.

The 'stuff luff' system has already been mentioned and undoubtedly gives the highest degree of control of draft position on a dinghy jib.

The rules for many classes dictate that the luff wire shall be fixed at both ends, which means using the conventional luff wire system lashed at the head.

Windows

Crash, collision or vision windows are very useful when you are attempting to line up on a hectic start line, but sailors often worry that putting a window in the sail will affect the cloth stretch in that area. Fitted correctly, windows should make very little difference to the sail shape, as they are generally positioned in low-load areas near the luff or foot. Nevertheless, avoid asking for windows in the luff of heavy air jibs, as used on the J24 or Soling; these are subject to high halyard loadings, and some local distortion above the window may result.

Some regatta sailors of boats with large genoas also fit a 'pre-start window' below the collision window near the foot, so that when the sail is flying high and loose before the start, vision is not reduced at the critical moment.

If permitted, another useful window can be incorporated in the luff of the mainsail just below the spreaders. Positioned correctly, this spreader window provides the crew with a ready visual guide as to how far in the headsail leech is trimmed against the reference point of the spreaders. This is particularly useful on trapeze dinghies and keelboats, where boatspeed is sacrificed by climbing down from the high side to look under the boom and check the jib sheeting.

Special fittings

Most boats have one or two non-standard fittings which may require minor changes to the cut of the sail.

One critical measurement to check is the knock-back at the tack of the mainsail. This is the distance from the aft side of the mast to the tack pin. If the amount of knock-back does not fit your spars, the sail will always set with a crease. Too much is better than too little, as an extra shackle can easily be added to give a smooth fit. Alternatively,

Left: Collision window in the jib and main. Above: A spreader window in the main. This helps the crew on the windward side check the genoa sheeting in relation to the spreader.

a simple lashing provides an easily adjustable solution.

For boats using a stuff luff system on the jib, some system is required for tensioning the luff. A small cleat mounted by the tack is one option, allowing adjustment on the water.

If your boat has a spinnaker chute you will need a retrieval patch on the sail, or possibly two if it is a large sail in a short chute. Some keelboat sailors use a swivel shackle on the spinnaker head and Englefield clips taped onto the clew rings. Launching a spinnaker from the cockpit in a Soling or Dragon is made easier by folding the sail into a tight bundle, secured by a Velcro tab. When needed the sail is thrown out of the cockpit in the bundle; by striking the sheet and guy when the sail is half hoisted, the sail sets straight away and well clear of the rig.

Below and right: Measuring mast pre-bend against a straight string stretched between the black bands.

Development classes

If you sail a development class you will have many more options to discuss with the sailmaker. Most sail lofts will have developed a preferred specification for such boats, including a recommended sail area distribution for main and jib. Minor variations from the sailmaker's standard dimensions can be accommodated without problem, but if you ask him to change his sail area ratios dramatically, then you will be moving away from the carefully developed and proven sail shapes.

However, whichever class you sail, it is well worth reading the class rules to check out the full range of rig options allowed. You may find, for example, that the jib is only limited to a maximum

sail area, in which case you could have a tall, thin sail or a short, wide one.

The tall, thin jib is definitely faster upwind, especially on flat water, but downwind in choppy conditions a lower-aspect sail is quicker in marginal planing conditions. This may well be because the lower-aspect sail is easier to set and read offwind.

So if you mainly race inland try using a high-aspect sail, but if you are sailing in a regatta circuit of predominantly coastal venues you may decide to opt for the more conventional lower-aspect sail.

WHAT THE SAILMAKER SHOULD TELL YOU

Many sailmakers issue a tuning leaflet with their sails with basic guidelines for setting up the rig. The tuning guide should provide you with the following information to coarse-tune the rig.

Mast pre-bend

The amount of pre-bend which the mainsail luff is cut to fit is measured with rig tension applied but without the sail rigged. The reading is taken at spreader height from the aft side of the mast to a straight string stretched from black band to black band. The mast is pre-bent by angling the spreaders aft, increasing their length and increasing rig tension.

Rake

The degree of fore and aft rake suited to the sails is commonly measured by hoisting a tape to the head of the mast on the main halyard, and measuring off at the intersection of the deck and the transom, or hull and transom.

Forestay tension

Forestay tension controls the amount of leeward

Below and right: Measuring mast rake: log the distance from the upper black band to the top of the transom (or to the intersection between the transom and the floor).

forestay sag which in turn affects pointing ability. The sailmaker cuts the jib's luff hollow to accommodate a certain degree of forestay sag and it is vital to set the boat up with a corresponding rig tension. This is best measured using a tension meter.

Spreader length

Your sailmaker should give you guide to spreader length and deflection, which will provide a useful starting point for setting up the rig. Your crew weight will determine whether you then shorten or lengthen them. In general, the longer the spreaders the stiffer the mast will be held sideways. However, if the spreaders are too long the leech will not open up when you're overpowered, and the mast will be pushed to leeward and pump sideways in a strong breeze.*

WHICH SAILS?

The size of your sail inventory will depend on the size of your boat and your budget, and the range of conditions you are likely to encounter. For most dinghy classes the sails are all-purpose and choice is a question of which design or make. With keelboats you are often faced with a choice of light, heavy or all-purpose sails for both main and jib. This can create a dilemma when you are allowed to measure in only two of each at a regatta.

Below and below right: Measuring the rig tension. Using a tension meter, pull the pointer to the mark and then read where the centre of the shroud cuts the scale. Finally use the chart on the back of the meter to convert to kilograms or pounds. In this case the tension is 255 kg (560lb).

For example, consider the options if you race a Dragon.

Club Racing:
- General purpose mainsail, 0 – 25 knots.
- Medium/heavy genoa, 8 – 25 knots, with fine entry for optimum pointing ability.
- All-purpose tri-radial spinnaker.

Club racing and open events:
- General purpose mainsail.
- Flat, medium/heavy genoa.
- Full, medium/heavy genoa, for choppy sea conditions.
- Optional light-air genoa, 0 – 12 knots.
- All-purpose tri-radial spinnaker.

International regatta circuit:
- General purpose mainsail.
- Heavy-air mainsail, 23 knots plus.
- Light-air genoa, 0 – 12 knots.
- Flat medium/heavy genoa.
- Full medium/heavy genoa.
- Tri-radial reaching spinnaker.
- Radial head running spinnaker.

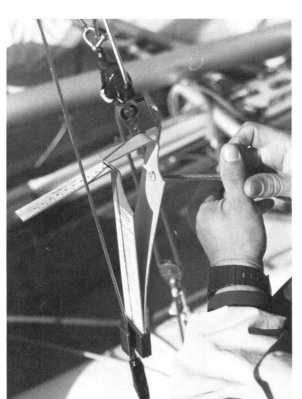

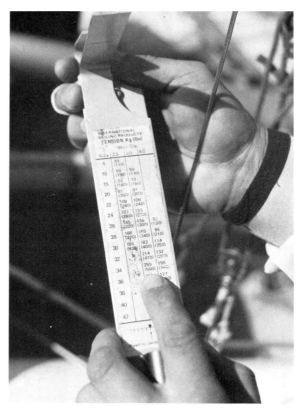

Mylar or Dacron

Mylar is often the best fabric for building headsails, but it is not always ideal for dinghy mainsails, where a certain amount of stretch is generally required. Where Mylar does score over Dacron is in the greater range of panel constructions it permits. Compared to Dacron, there is a much larger range of 'warp orientated' fabrics available (fabrics strongest in the long, warp direction) in Mylar. This means that it is often possible to build leech-cut or radial Mylar sails which could not be cut from Dacron as no suitable warp cloth is available.

Properly looked after a Mylar sail should last a little longer than a yarn-tempered sail. Where a Dacron sail will stretch a little every time it is hoisted, but retain some elasticity, a Mylar sail will stretch very little until it reaches the point at which the fabric is overloaded. Thereafter, the Mylar permanently deforms and the sail suddenly becomes uncompetitive. This is why you will often see a maximum windspeed stamped on the clew of a Mylar genoa. As long as the sailmaker selects the correct cloth weight for a given windspeed and the owner takes care not to exceed that range, a Mylar sail should enjoy a long life.

Below: Measuring spreader deflection: put a straight edge across the spreader tips and measure from it to the back of the mast.

'Hi-tech' constructions

Radial panel constructions are a very strong method of engineering a sail. Radial panels have become the standard configuration on offshore boats in recent years, and they are now increasingly common among the one-design classes.

The first steps towards building radial sails were made during the 12-metre campaigns of 1983. Computer-generated stress maps showed that a sail's maximum loading was in the leech area, travelling in an arc between head and clew. By referring to such stress maps sailmakers were able to align warp-orientated fabrics with the sail loading; the result was the radial configuration.

Above: The maximum wind speed for this Mylar genoa is 22 knots.

The vertical radial panels originate from the head and clew, meeting in a joining seam at roughly two-thirds height. The vertical leech panels dramatically reduce leech stretch, while the overall arrangement allows the clew loads to follow the thread lines in the cloth as they spread into the sail. Some sail lofts create the shape within the radial seams, employing computers to calculate the broadseam required. Others use straight seams to join the radial panels and then put the shape into the sail using traditional horizontal seams. This latter system somewhat reduces the benefits of the radial construction as any seams that cross the leech will result in a certain amount of stretch.

As the radial construction results in a stronger sail the cloth weight can be relatively lighter than a conventional cross-cut sail. The reinforcement patches can also be reduced, resulting in a lighter all up weight which allows the sail to tack faster and set more easily in lighter airs.

*See Tuning your Dinghy, *Lawrie Smith, Fernhurst Books.*

4 Sail setting

Sail setting is a two-stage process: fitting the sails to the boat, and setting them up using the sail shaping controls.

FITTING

When you try the sails on the boat for the first time, it is important to check their dimensions. The mainsail should set between the black bands on mast and boom when the halyard and outhaul are fully tensioned. If the sail appears short in the foot or luff, ease the tension in the sewn-in bolt rope. Tensioned too tightly the bolt rope can

Right: Lashing the tack cringle carefully allows the sail to set without creases. Below and below right: This Finn takes the idea further; an adjustable inhaul effectively alters the shape of the luff curve in the lower third of the sail. Pulling the tack forward adds luff curve.

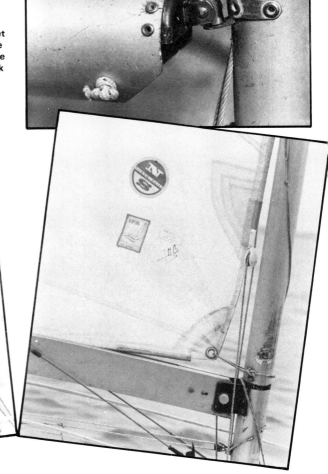

prevent the sails from being pulled out to the bands. Don't worry if the jib luff measures close to the minimum: headsails are often laid out to the minimum luff but maximum leech length in order to get the clew as low as possible, so enhancing the end plate effect.

Fixing the tack

Tie or pin the mainsail tack in position with the right amount of knock-back, so that the sail sets without creases.

Shackle the headsail onto the forward part of the bow fitting at a height that allows the foot to sweep the deck. If your boat is fitted with tack horns, as on the J24, you need to ignore them and attach the tack ring to a central shackle. This arrangement allows the sail to set in the same lead position on both tacks, whereas using the tack horns involves different sheeting positions for each side of the boat.

Battens

When fitting the battens, ensure that the ends push back hard against the leech. Check they are fully captive within their pockets and not just caught inside the leech tape.

Boats with a full-length top batten (one that butts up against the mast) such as the 420, 470 and 505, will require a stiff batten for heavy air and a softer one of around 3.5lbs (1.5kg) compression for medium conditions. It may also be necessary to vary the stiffness of the tapered battens lower down the sail. In a strong breeze the bottom two battens need to be stiff in order to hold the leech straight and flat, and to prevent the sail from inverting.

The lightest battens are of the foam-cored variety; sleeved in glass on two sides. These battens tend to develop their maximum bend at 30% aft of the tip, rather further forward than usual; this allows more fullness to be carried in the head of the sail in medium conditions.

If the inboard end of the batten creates local creases in the sail, try replacing the end caps with tape.

SAIL CONTROLS

When you are satisfied that the sails are properly fitted, you can begin setting them up using the various controls.

Mastbend

Mastbend is the main device used for setting the amount of fullness in the mainsail and controlling the degree of forestay tension.

The mast should be set up with a prescribed degree of pre-bend to match the luff curve the sailmaker has put into the sail, but further pre-bending by rig tension is necessary when there is insufficient wind to cause the mast to bend naturally and achieve the designed depth, draft and leech shape.

As the breeze gets up, bend the mast more than the initial pre-bend by a) removing the chocks in front of the mast; b) angling the spreader tips aft; c) increasing the rig tension. This will serve to flatten out the top two-thirds of the sail by increasing the distance from leech to luff. (On the other hand a dead straight mast will give you the deepest, most powerful sail shape.) Bending the mast also loosens off the leech, because the distance from mast tip to clew has been decreased. The draft position will tend to move aft as the sail is flattened off.

Left: Adjust the height of the jib tack so the foot of the sail sweeps the deck.

Above: The effect of luff tension on a Soling jib. (Left) halyard too tight – draft 35% aft. (Right) perfect – draft 42.5% aft. (Centre) halyard too loose – draft 45% aft.

Luff tension

A sail's draft position (the point of maximum depth) is controlled by the amount of tension on the luff. As more tension is applied to the luff, the draft point moves forward, from around 50% when completely slack to 30 – 35% aft of the leading edge when full on.

Many sailors get this the wrong way round, believing that the harder they pull the halyard the flatter the front of the sail will become. To convince yourself that the draft really does move forward, try repeatedly hauling on luff tension and then letting it go; you will soon see the way the maximum depth slides forward and back in the sail. The best way to observe this is to lie in the boat and look up the mainsail from underneath the boom while someone else pumps the halyard a few times. Try to picture the depth and draft position in percentage terms. Once you have determined where the draft position is in the sail, you should become familiar with locating it from your normal sailing position.

Below: The cunningham pulls the draft forward in the main. A secondary effect is to open the top of the leech. (Left) cunningham on. (Right) cunningham off.

In practice mainsail luff tension is controlled by a combination of the halyard and the cunningham, which can be thought of as an additional tensioning device for use once the sail has been pulled up to the black bands, and which allows easy adjustment for upwind and downwind legs. Most dinghies use wire halyards to reduce stretch, which hook onto a rack, highfield lever or muscle-box. These systems provide for basic light or heavy air settings, while the cunningham provides the fine tune.

A greater range of luff tension is often required on keelboats, and this is governed by how tight the halyard is set. Most boats of this size use a small winch to wind up the tension. When running downwind in light airs, for example, it is common practice to ease the mainsail down the mast a few inches to produce a smoother and fuller shape near the luff.

The role of the cunningham

As the breeze gets up and the mainsail is stretched out to the black bands, the draft will move aft to around 55% as a result of the increased loading on the sailcloth. With the draft in this position the

Below and below left: The effect of the clew outhaul. (Left) outhaul eased – note the curve in the foot of the sail and the closed leech in this area. (Right) tensioning the outhaul has the opposite effect.

sail is very prone to stall and provides little power in a chop. It is the job of the cunningham to pull the draft back to its designed position: around 44% back from the luff.

An important secondary action of the cunningham is to free off the upper leech, depowering the sail, which in turn reduces the amount of weather helm.

Outhaul

The outhaul is used to set the required amount of depth in the lower third of the mainsail. This varies with the amount of breeze, and is altered for upwind and downwind legs. A particularly efficient outhaul system for trapeze boats incorporates a lever set under the boom for throwing off a fixed amount of outhaul for the reach, but also includes a clam cleat for fine adjustment of the upwind position. The crew has only a few seconds inside the boat when tacking and it is much faster to simply knock off a lever than it is to ease a line out through a cleat. If the foot rope is elasticated the clew will move forward of its own accord when released, opening up the shelf foot to give a full reaching shape.

The outhaul also has an effect on lower leech tension. Easing the clew firms up the leech below the bottom batten quite significantly.

Mainsheet

The mainsheet controls the amount of twist in the leech. A closed or tight leech is one with little twist, with the top batten parallel to the end of the boom. Easing the mainsheet allows the boom to rise up and puts more twist into the top of the sail. This open leech allows the air to escape more freely from the top of the sail, creating less drag and less sideways force.

Main traveller

The traveller is used to position the boom relative to the centreline of the boat. As such the traveller is closely involved with mainsheet tension and the

Right: The effect of the mainsheet. (Top) tight mainsheet reduces twist and improves pointing. (Right) easing the mainsheet a few centimetres twists off the leech for extra power in light airs and depowers the sail in heavy airs.

action of the two controls should be considered together. The traveller has direct control over the size of the jib slot and the amount of weather helm. The traveller is eased to leeward with increasing wind strength in order to reduce weather helm. As a result, the slot between main and jib is reduced and the jib lead has to be moved outboard to compensate.

Kicking strap (vang)

The kicking strap or vang is used to bend the mast low down by forcing the boom forwards at the gooseneck, and is used to help flatten off the sail in heavy air. The vang can also be used instead of the mainsheet to set up the leech tension in strong winds, while the mainsheet is constantly used to adjust the angle of the boom. This technique is known as 'vang-sheeting' and is common practice among Laser sailors.

Downwind the vang is used to control the amount of twist in the main and prevents the top of the sail being blown forward of the mast.

Forestay tension

Forestay tension controls:
- The amount of fullness in the jib.
- The degree of pointing ability.

The forestay can sag off an enormous amount to leeward while sailing. This sag puts extra fullness into the jib, over and above that already cut into the sail; the result is that the boat loses pointing ability owing to the jib becoming very draft forward.

In practice, most high-performance dinghies such as the 470 use considerable forestay tension throughout most of the wind range because the hull is light and easily driven and a lack of pointing ability would be disastrous. However, heavier keelboats such as the Soling and Dragon require extra power in the front of the headsail in light winds, so it is usual to allow the forestay to sag several inches in these condtions.

Above: Jib luff sag, one of the main speed controls on a Soling, is to be avoided on most dinghies.

Below: Setting up the jib luff tension (see text).

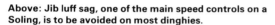

Jib luff tension

In the case of dinghy jibs the degree of luff tension is determined by how tightly the head cringle is lashed to the eye of the luff wire. Some class rules permit stuff luffs and a jib cunningham which allow the tension to be altered while sailing.

   To set the jib luff tension string up the sail

Top: Loosening the jib halyard on a Soling allows the flow to move aft and opens the leech.
Above: Tightening the halyard has the opposite effect, and can be used to completely close the top leech of the jib.

horizontally between two posts with the tension on the luff wire which you would use while sailing. With the tack eye fixed to the luff wire apply sufficient tension to the head of the sail to virtually remove the creases at the luff. This is your flat water, optimum pointing set-up. Tightening the head lashing even more pulls the draft further forward for power in choppy conditions where pointing ability is less important.

Keelboat headsails generally use a stretchy rope or a heavy luff tape, which allows the draft position to be determined directly via halyard tension. Tightening the luff pulls the head further away from the foot, which also tensions the leech. A few inches of halyard tension can completely close the top leech of a Dragon or Soling headsail. Any adjustment to the halyard should be accompanied by moving the jib leads upwards to maintain the original leech tension.

Jib sheeting position

The best advice on jib sheeting is to use a system which, while remaining within the the class rules, allows you the widest range of lead positions. The systems permitted by the rules may range from the fixed fairleads found on the Cadet to the athwartships travellers with barber haulers common on the Dragon.

Moving the jib leads fore and aft has a similar effect to sliding them up and down vertically. Moving the lead forward places more of the sheet

Below: The effect of the barber hauler. (Left) a loose barber hauler opens the jib leech. (Centre) as the barber hauler is pulled down the leech becomes tighter. (Right) a tight barber hauler produces a tight leech.

tension down the leech and less along the foot. This is a good starting point for medium airs, when a firm leech is required for good pointing ability, and when there is no danger of the mainsail being backwinded, because the boom is on the centreline.

As the breeze gets up the jib lead is pulled progressively aft, in order to flatten off the lower part of the sail and to free off the top of the leech. The open leech allows:
- The air to escape more freely from the sail.
- An increase in the size of the slot, allowing the main traveller to be eased down to leeward to balance the increasing weather helm experienced in a strong breeze.
- The boat to be sailed more upright as heeling forces are reduced.

When finding the correct jib lead position for a particular wind strength the telltales provide a useful rule of thumb. Luff gently just above close hauled, so that the windward telltales begin to lift. If the top telltale lifts before the bottom one, the lead is too far aft and needs to be moved forward or down. Conversely, move the leads aft or up if the bottom telltale lifts first. When all the telltales lift at the same moment the jib luff is at the same angle of incidence to the wind from head to tack and is trimmed perfectly.

Sheeting angles

When people talk about sheeting angles they are referring to the angle the jibsheet makes with the centre line. The optimum angle for good pointing is around eight degrees but depends on the hull shape and headsail size.

A non-overlapping jib can be sheeted much closer than a large genoa without causing the main to backwind.

The basic rule is to sheet as far inboard as possible without causing the sail to stall; this gives the best pointing ability. As the wind increases and the waves get up the tendency to stall increases and the jib has to be sheeted at a wider angle; this provides more speed at the expense of pointing and is known as 'footing'.

It is important to have as much control over the sheeting angle as the class rules permit. In the Cadet and 420 classes where the jib lead is fixed at a very wide angle the trick is to barber-haul the sheet closer in by pulling on the windward sheet. If you are allowed athwartships tracks fit them. However, if you wish to keep the layout simple use a single fore-and-aft track which is angled outwards at the back. Then as the lead is moved aft for heavy air the slot is opened up automatically.

SETTING UP THE SAILS

Having looked at each of the sail shaping controls and how they work, it is time to consider how to set up the sails for beating in medium wind conditions. The following directions may not apply exactly to your particular boat or rig, but should serve as a useful starting point for correct trim.

Mainsail

1   Set up the mast with the prescribed pre-bend using rig tension, spreaders and mast chocks.
2   Set the luff tension and cunningham so that small creases are just visible, and the draft is approximately 45% aft.
3   Stretch the foot out to within an inch or so of the black band.
4   Use the traveller to centre the boom on or slightly below the centreline, so that there is a small amount of weather helm.
5   Trim the mainsheet so that the outer end of the top batten is parallel with the end of the boom. Stitching coloured trim stripe over the pocket makes it more visible.

Jib

1   Tighten the forestay for optimum pointing.
2   Set the luff tension so the creases are just

removed (for flat water), and the draft is approximately 45% aft.
3   Set up the fore-and-aft sheeting so that the tell-tales all lift together.

CHANGING GEAR

You should always think of medium winds as maximum power conditions. Keep asking yourself throughout the race 'Can we handle more power now?' It is vital to have this question in your mind the whole time.

In keelboats it is easy for the helmsman to become locked into sailing the boat through the water, then look up and see that the boats to leeward have suddenly taken out a couple of lengths. In variable conditions one of the crew should be responsible for monitoring the rig constantly, and immediately the boat hits a lull the sails can be powered up to accommodate the change in windspeed.

The most obvious effects of a lull are:
•   The mainsail leech appears completely closed, and the top batten may be pointing a few degrees above the centreline.
•   The genoa leech, previously trimmed two inches off the spreaders, is just touching and the leech appears closed.
•   The genoa foot is creased up around the shrouds at deck level.
•   The boat is heeled less.
The crew's instant reaction should be to ease sheets a little to put the twist back into both sails.

Changes for light air

To power up the rig:
1   Straighten the mast to add depth to mainsail. In a dinghy add chocks in front of the mast. In a keelboat ease the runner or backstay tension.
2   Open the mainsail leech so the top telltale flies most of the time (Ease mainsheet and/or vang).
3   Pull the traveller to weather, to position the boom on the centreline for maximum pointing ability.
4   Add depth to the lower third of the mainsail. (Ease the clew outhaul two inches).
5   Add depth to the jib. (Move the lead forward and ease the sheet to keep the leech tension constant and twist off the upper leech.)
6   Move the jib lead to the maximum inboard position to improve pointing.

Heavy airs   Medium airs   Light airs

	Heavy airs	**Medium airs**	**Light airs**
Strut	up	down	up
Vang	hard	just tensioned	off
Cunningham	on	off	off
Mainsheet	just off	hard in	off (boom on quarter)
Outhaul	on	on	eased slightly
Jibsheet	ease	tight	ease
Barber-hauler	up	down	halfway

Changes for heavy air

The time to depower the rig is generally more evident than the need to make light air adjustments. In a blow the crew struggle to keep the boat flat and the boat moves sideways with each gust. The mainsail looks deep, the draft is too far aft and there is too much weather helm. To depower the rig:

1   Increase mast bend. (On a dinghy remove chocks in front of the mast and use the vang to promote bend low down. On a keelboat tighten the runners and/or backstay, and tighten the vang.

2   Pull the draft forward for more drive through the waves (pull on the cunningham).

3   Open the top of the leech to depower the sail and reduce weather helm. (On a dinghy pull on the cunningham. On a keelboat pull on the backstay.)

4   Flatten the base of the mainsail (pull the clew outhaul out to the black band).

5   Reduce forestay sag. (On a dinghy increase rig tension. On a keelboat increase runner tension.)

6   Ease the diamonds (if fitted) to allow the topmast to fall off to leeward and open up the leech of the main. (This is effective on Contenders and Dragons).

5 Spinnakers

Unlike a fore-and-aft sail a spinnaker is often stalled over most of its area while it is flying. Even when close reaching, attached flow is present over only 60% of the sail. However, in some respects the spinnaker does behave like a genoa in that the draft can be pulled forward with luff tension, and the leech can be twisted open by raising the clew.

On the run

For running downwind, the spinnaker should be as big as possible, and set so as to achieve the maximum projected area to the wind. On a dead run the apparent wind is in the same direction as the true wind and the air is almost completely stalled in the sail. Because of this it is always faster to sail a few degrees closer to the wind and develop some airflow across the sail. To maximise the projected area flatten off the sail and pull back the pole (and ease out the sheet) to set as much of the spinnaker as possible out of the main's windshadow.

Reaching

The size and shape of the spinnaker is much more important on the reach. The deeper the middle of the sail the more power it produces, but at the expense of area. Pole height and angle are the two most critical controls when flying the spinnaker on the reach.

The sail should be full in the head to provide enough lift, so that it sets as far away from the rig as possible and does not backwind the main.

Choice of spinnaker

One-design spinnakers should be built to maximum luff and foot lengths but not necessarily to maximum mid-girth width. The amount of leeway allowed in the spinnaker mid-girth (S.M.G.) will depend on the class rules, but it is commonly around 100 mm.

Small, narrow spinnakers can often be faster on close reaches. The reason is that with maxi spinnakers the slot between the spinnaker leech and mainsail is small; this means the main has to be overtrimmed to avoid backwinding, which cuts boat speed.

On an Olympic course, the gains possible on the reaches with a smaller spinnaker can often outweigh the loss of speed on the run in both very light breezes and heavy weather.

When running downwind, a portion of the spinnaker is always hidden behind the main. In light airs this area does not fill and contributes zero lift. The sail is dragged down and prevented from filling properly. In heavy air the smaller kite is more stable to trim, there is less sail in the lee of the main, and the tendency to oscillate from side to side (known as the death roll), is reduced.

However, when broad reaching or running in medium air, the maximum-size spinnaker will generally be faster. Your choice of spinnaker will be a compromise based on the following factors:
- The type of course sailed.
- The number of spinnakers which can be carried under the class rules.
- The crew weight.

Matching the spinnaker to the race course

The Fireball and 470 classes illustrate the factors to be considered when matching spinnaker size to the type of course. Traditionally, Fireballs use a close-reaching course with a 60 degree gybe rather than the 90 degree gybe found on an Olympic course. As a result, small spinnakers have tended to predominate.

In the 470 class the question of size is a little more subjective. For the old Olympic course of two triangles, the majority of spinnakers were cut to the minimum S.M.G. with a few halfway

Above: A tri-radial spinnaker. The seams radiate from the head and clews.

Above: A cross-cut spinnaker. The seams are at right angles to the leeches.

between minimum and maximum. However, with the change in the Olympic course to only one triangle and a longer beat it seems in practice that the committee often fail to lay the gybe mark far enough from marks 1 and 3. The result is that the reaches become broader than 90 degrees. If this is the case, the fastest spinnaker is a sail laid out to halfway between minimum and maximum S.M.G.

More than one sail

If you think deciding the size of a 470 spinnaker is hard, try a Soling! In this class, you are allowed two large spinnakers and one small one. A typical Soling spinnaker inventory is:
* Tri-radial reacher, S.M.G. maximum or just less, built in 0.75oz resinated Nylon such as Dynac or HST to withstand stretch.
* Cross-cut runner, maximum S.M.G. with large shoulders, cut from a softer 0.75oz Nylon such as Stabilkote to permit some stretch.
* Radial head mini spinnaker for use as an all-purpose heavy-air sail and light air runner, cut from 0.75oz resinated Nylon.

Tri-radials

While the majority of dinghies use cross-cut spinnakers most keelboats use the tri-radial construction for reaching spinnakers because the extra loading caused by the heavy displacement would cause a cross-cut sail to distort dramatically.

The purpose of the radial panel layout is the same as that of a radial-cut genoa. By aligning the strong thread lines in the cloth with the load lines in the sail, and by reducing the number of horizontal seams, cloth and seam stretch is reduced considerably. Cloth stretch can be further reduced by use of highly resinated or stabilised fabrics such as Dynac or HST.

This choice of cloth and construction produces a sail which will maintain, as far as possible, its designed shape under the high loads encountered on a close reach. If you use only one spinnaker on your particular class of keelboat, and you are principally interested in club racing around the cans, then the tri-radial will provide the best all-round performance and the longest competitive lifespan.

Cross-cuts

A cross-cut spinnaker is often preferred as a running sail. Large shoulders can be built onto a cross-cut and this is not possible on a tri-radial. On the run the strength of the tri-radial is no longer required as the sail's loading decreases with the apparent windspeed. Because cloth and seam stretch are less of a problem, softer and sometimes lighter Nylon can be used. As the softer Nylon includes less resin, its actual weight is less than the more stabilised cloths. This allows the sail to set more readily in light airs.

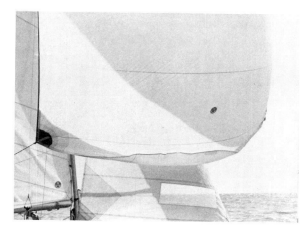

Above: A spherical cut spinnaker. The seams are at right angles to the centreline although there is no centre seam.

Dinghy cross-cuts

The reasons why dinghy spinnakers are generally cross-cut are:
- The reduced loads experienced by a dinghy sail do not warrant the tri-radial construction.
- It is possible to build shoulders on to the sail.
- In some cases, cloth stretch can be used to good effect.
- Cross-cut spinnakers are simpler and less expensive to build and develop.

There are two forms of cross-cut spinnaker. The true cross-cut has the panels arranged at right-angles to the leeches, and has a centre seam or 'mitre' down the middle. On the water the head panels appear to be cut in a chevron pattern. The alternative form of horizontal-panelled spinnaker is called the spherical-cut. This has no centre seam and the panels are aligned at right-angles to the centre fold instead of the leeches.

The major difference between the two is that the leeches will open much more on the spherical sail, as the cloth in the leech is orientated along the stretchy bias direction. The leech of the true cross-cut is orientated parallel to the stronger fill fibres, which are capable of withstanding higher loading.

There have been some very successful spherical-cut Flying Dutchman spinnakers, built from a soft and stretchy nylon. Cut to be relatively deep and full, the sail provides good power and lift on the broad reach and run. On heading up on a tight reach, the loads increase considerably on the sail, resulting in the luff stretching out flat and the leech twisting open more. Thus the sail is able to change shape automatically to suit the reaching and running legs.

Radial head

The radial head spinnaker is, if you like, a hybrid between a tri-radial and a spherical-cut. The radial panels in the head reduce stretch and control shape in the top of the sail, while the bottom is allowed to stretch a little more to create a deeper shape. This type of construction is little used these days, but has specialised applications

Above: A radial-head spinnaker.

on small keelboats, for example the mini spinnaker used on the Soling; it is also often used for Dragon running spinnakers.

Crew weight

Everything else being equal, a heavy crew can carry a larger spinnaker than lightweights. But it's seldom that everything else *is* equal, and spinnaker size is better determined by the skill of the crew.

Above: Tie the sheet close to the spinnaker clew, so the sail can be pulled right up to the pole.

Spinnaker fittings

On a dinghy you should use 5mm Kevlar for the spinnaker sheets, with a soft 8mm or 10mm tail for easy handling. The sheets should be tied directly to the sail to save the weight of clips or shackles, and to keep the distance between the pole-end and the corner of the sail to a minimum. If the boat has a chute you will require a retrieval patch in the centre of the sail, at least ten inches (25cm) in diameter. If the spinnaker sock is particularly short or the sail relatively large, it may pay to fit two puller patches. The lower patch should have a small cringle through which the retrieval line passes, up to the second patch, where it is tied onto a webbing loop. When the sail is doused, it is first retracted to less than half its original length, and it is then much quicker to pull it down into the sock.

On keelboats with more than one spinnaker, some form of clip or snap-shackle is unavoidable. 'Sister' or 'union' clips are used by many sailors;

they are fine until they become a little worn, when there is a danger that they may shake loose. Snap-shackles are a safer choice, especially for higher load applications, but be sure to choose a light but sufficiently strong model of minimum overall length.

In the Soling and Dragon the spinnaker can be launched from the cockpit, rolled into a tight bundle and secured by a Velcro tab. The package is thrown clear of the rig and hoisted halfway before a sharp tug on the guy causes the parcel to explode and the kite to set instantly. The system ensures that the sail is set fast and well away from the rig, minimising the chances of the spinnaker becoming ripped or twisted during the hoist.

When using both reaching and running kites on an Olympic course there is normally no need to repack a sail as the reacher is used for the first triangle only. The running sail is then ready for launching on the downward leg. Occasionally a major windshift on the first lap may necessitate using the runner first, so keep a laundry basket or launching turtle on board in case you need to repack and launch the sail again.

With more than one spinnaker in the boat it is as well to have each one clearly marked on the corners to avoid clipping on the wrong sail when you are in a hurry.

Above: On a boat like the Soling, where more than one spinnaker is carried, use small, light, strong plastic snapshackles.

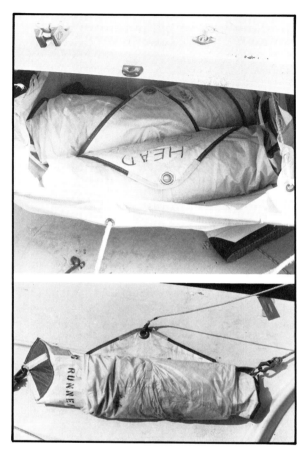

Above: A Soling spinnaker is rolled into a bundle, secured with a Velcro tab, and stored in a launching bag.
Below: At the launch the spinnaker is lifted out of the bag, thrown outboard and hoisted halfway before the guy is struck to open the parcel.

FLYING THE SPINNAKER (REACHING)

On the reach, set the pole height so that the spinnaker curls first halfway up the luff. If the sail breaks first below this point move the pole down; if above, move the pole up. The two clews should be approximately level, with the pole set horizontally on the mast if possible. Keep watching for the wind to shift aft and then move the pole back as far as possible. The sheet should be played continuously so that the luff is always on the curl. Get into a rhythm of slowly easing the sheet out until the luff just breaks and then pulling it in. The sheet should never stop moving.

The time to pump the sail is when you feel a good surfing wave roll under the stern. The bow will dip and that is the moment for two or three sharp pumps on the sheet and guy to lift the bow up onto the wave. Remember, under I.Y.R.U. rule 54.3 you are allowed no more than three pumps per wave, and only when planing conditions exist.

Close reaching

The main aim when close reaching is to keep the slot between the spinnaker leech and mainsail as wide and as open as possible. If the slot is too small, the main will have to be overtrimmed, stalling the sail dramatically. In order to keep the slot open, try to keep the sail as far away from the boat as possible:
● Set the pole horizontally. If class rules permit, fit an extra eye on the mast above the standard one, or an adjustable track system.

Above: The pole is too high – the luff curls first below the half height.

Above: The pole is too low – the luft curls first above the half height.

● In medium conditions, let the spinnaker halyard off to move the head of the sail away from the mast.
● Let the twinning line off to encourage the leech to twist off and to help position the clew as

far to leeward as possible. The main boom then becomes the limiting factor on clew height, so

Below: On a light air run lower the pole to reduce the amount of unsupported area.

Below: Close reaching in brisk conditions.

Above: When the pole height is correct the luff breaks evenly as the sheet is eased.

ease the vang until the top batten becomes almost too open.

When using the small spinnaker in heavy airs many Soling crews allow the spinnaker sheet to ride up over the boom; this allows the leech to twist off sufficiently to keep the boat upright.

Running

When running in light airs there is insufficient wind to lift the spinnaker to its normal flying position, so the pole should be lowered to reduce the amount of unsupported area. The sail will then set more readily and provide a much greater projected area. As soon as there is enough breeze to lift the spinnaker, the pole should be moved up so that the clews are level and the pole horizontal. As before, the prime objective is to provide the maximum projected area, so bring the pole aft as soon as the wind has moved astern.

To keep the outboard end of the pole steady, the guy should be held down firmly near the shrouds by a hook or twinning line. Pulling the twinning line down after the gybe effectively pulls the guy further aft, so be sure to compensate by easing the guy before cleating it.

In heavy air the leeward twinning line is sometimes pulled on to prevent the sail from oscillating. In any case pull it on to make the sail more controllable when gybing. In strong winds the pole should be lifted to help the air escape from the top of the sail. If all the boats around you are broaching, try over-squaring the pole a little to flatten off the foot. But beware of over-doing it; if the chute collapses in heavy air it will start to flog and can take a long time to fill again.

Below: Running under spinnaker. (Left) the pole is too high. (Centre) the pole is too low. (Right) the pole is the right height for running in medium airs.

6   Fault finder

It is essential to recognise when a sail is not working correctly. Having isolated a fault, it is often possible to make changes in the rig adjustment to achieve correct trim. If the sail still does not look right it may need to be returned to the sailmaker for alteration.

MAINSAIL FAULTS

Luff curve does not fit mast bend

The most common fault sailmakers have to deal with is a luff curve which does not match the mast bend. Spotting the lack (or over-abundance) of luff curve is basically a matter of getting your eye in.

If the sail has too much luff curve the cloth will be tightly wrinkled just behind the mast because there is too much there. The mast needs to be pulled forward at this point to take the wrinkles away. This is achieved by pre-bending the mast a little more. An easy way on boats without adjustable spreaders is to move the heel of the mast back slightly, while keeping it fully chocked at deck level.

In the case of luff curve starvation the sail comes out very tight, like a board, from the back of the mast. There is just not enough cloth there, and there will be a crease running from clew to luff.

The first step in curing this is to try to reduce the amount of pre-bend. However, this may not

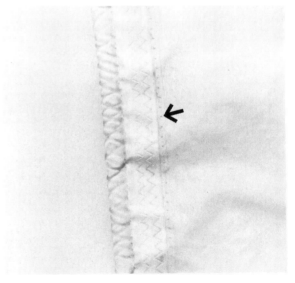

Left: Insufficient luff curve in this sail is causing wrinkles.
Above: This luff has been 'let out' to get more curve, leaving a telltale line of holes (arrowed).

always be desirable. Furthermore the luff curve may only require altering over a small area in order to match a particular mast's characteristics. In eight out of ten cases of sails not matching the mast, it is because the sail was originally designed around a different mast section.

Before getting the sail altered, take careful note of exactly how far up the mast the creases occur, or better still, take photographs in order to help the sailmaker judge how much alteration is required.

Finn sailors should be experts at spotting a fair luff curve, as it is a vital ingredient of a fast Finn sail. Finn masts are also notoriously individual, and the sail often has to be cut differently for each particular mast.

Loose leech

If the mainsail leech flutters upwind, try increasing the mainsheet tension or taking up some leechline (if fitted). When the mainsheet is hard on and the leech is still too loose (a common complaint with old sails which have stretched) the sail will flutter in between the battens.

Below: Mainsail leeches: loose (left) and tight (right).

To cure the problem note where the worst flutter occurs and then ask the sailmaker to put a few take-ups in the leech seams. This involves undoing the seam for about eight inches (20 cm) from the leech, moving the panels a few millimetres closer together and then reseaming.

If the leech now looks fine in light airs but continues to flutter in a breeze, the problem can often lie within the cloth. Perhaps surprisingly, one reason the leech does not stand firm is insufficient bias stretch – in other words the cloth is too firm in the 45 degree direction. This lack of stretch creates a flat leech which hinges open too soon. The only solution is to have a new sail made out of a cloth with greater bias stretch, this will produce a more rounded leech with a tight trailing edge.

Tight leech

Too tight a leech is a less common problem, but sometimes occurs in boats like 470s, where using normal mainsheet tension causes insufficient twist at the top batten. The cure is simply the reverse of a leech take-up: a let-out of a few millimetres at the offending seam.

Batten poke

Long creases running up the sail along the inboard ends of the battens are generally caused by too much batten poke. The sail has been cut with too much roach; this creates a sizeable compressive load, forcing the batten inwards into the sail. You can prove this is the cause if, when you pull the leech aft a few inches, the creases disappear.

Excessive batten poke usually occurs at the bottom batten, where the leech loads are greatest. It is for this reason that sails carry very little roach in that area. If your sail has too much roach it is a simple matter for your sailmaker to reduce it (although you do lose sail area).

Minor creasing at the batten ends can sometimes be solved by replacing bulky batten end fittings with tape.

Creases

No sail looks good with large creases running across it. A common complaint is 'over-bend creases' which run from the clew to just below the spreaders. These are caused by the mast bending too much in the lower section, pulling luff curve out of the sail and causing a line of tension from the clew. The solution is to either straighten the lower mast with extra chocks, or add more luff curve to the front of the sail.

Small creases originating from the clew patch but only carrying a few inches into the sail are due to cloth stretch in this high-load area. Better engineering of the reinforcement patch should prevent such creases.

Draft in wrong position

Draft position can be easily shifted from the 35% to 50% position through manipulation of luff tension. However, if your sail has the draft located at 20% aft when the luff tension is off, you have a problem! The sail will have very poor pointing ability, and in the case of a mainsail will show excessive backwinding. Unfortunately the cure involves major surgery to each broadseam, to move the point of maximum camber further aft.

Below: Jib leeches: a hooked leech (left) and a fluttering leech (right).

You can measure the exact draft position for yourself by photographing the sail from below. Lie in the bottom of the boat, and use a camera with a wide-angle lens, angled diagonally in order to get as much of the leech and luff in as possible. Check that the sail is sheeted correctly and is not luffing when you take the shot.

When you get the prints back draw the chord line in carefully, joining up the two ends of the trim stripe from leech to luff. (You can use the seams as trim stripes if none are present). With the chord line drawn in, move the ruler down the photo, holding it at right angles to the chord line (by sliding it along a set square) to find the position of maximum depth. Once you have found this point on the curve, join it with a line at right angles to the chord. This point now gives you the draft position and you can calculate the percentage draft position as shown in chapter 1. Similarly the depth can be measured and is also converted to a percentage of the total chord length.

Armed with this information, the sailmaker can evaluate the sail quickly and precisely, and he can

Below: Adding extra leech hollow.

decide if it is worth trying to recut it or not. Possibilities include altering the broadseam and changing the luff curve.

A feature of old sails is that the draft moves aft as the cloth breaks down and the bias stretch increases. For a while extra cunningham tension will help pull the draft forward to the original position.

JIB FAULTS

Hooked leach

If the jib leech has a significant hook to windward in light air this will increase drag and backwinding. (Any hook will blow out if the wind is strong enough). If the sail includes a leechline, the first step is to ensure that it is fully freed off. If the sail still hooks it is generally a sign of too much tension in the leech, often caused by the leech tape being too tight or the tape shrinking.

If the jib is new, it is worth asking the sail loft to fit a new leech tape and/or reduce the amount of leech hollow. However, the factors affecting jib leech curl are very critical, and it is not always an easy problem to solve.

As always the amount of leech tension placed in the sail through leech hollow is a compromise between too much, which causes the leech to hook, and too little, causing the leech to flutter. The firmer the cloth, the easier it is to produce a nice straight leech.

Old sails often develop a hooked leech as a result of cloth breakdown. To increase the life of the sail, the sailmaker can cut away the worn area by adding more leech hollow.

Jib leech flutter

Genoa or jib leeches will invariably flutter and vibrate at some point as the wind increases, due to cloth stretch. If your sail doesn't have a leech line and it begins to flutter very early in the wind range, the answer is to have some more hollow cut into the leech. This is a simple job, and in conjunction with a few leech take-ups can successfully rejuvenate an old and tired jib and curtail the fluttering.

Entry too fine

In the interests of improved performance to windward, headsails are being cut with finer and finer entries in an effort to improve pointing ability. These sails are what US sailors call 'fine groove': the margin between the sail luffing and the leeward side stalling is very small. Fine groove sails are great if you are a top helmsman sailing in flat water, but they often prove difficult to use in the majority of conditions.

Pulling the draft forward with luff tension will ease the problem, but will do little to change the actual luff angle of the sail. The best solution is to reduce the luff hollow by getting the sailmaker to put more cloth into the front of the genoa.

Conversely, if the front of the sail appears very full and the competition regularly points higher, you need to have more hollow cut into the luff.

SPINNAKER FAULTS

Shoulders fall in and collapse

To make the sail as large as possible, cross-cut spinnakers are cut with big 'shoulders' in the top. Shoulders are similar to the roach on a mainsail and need to be supported if the sail is to stand up in all conditions. To support large shoulders, the sail has to be cut quite flat in the top and this often results in creases radiating downwards from the head.

If the sail is designed to have large shoulders some creasing is inevitable, but if the shoulders are built too big without sufficient support from the body of the sail, the luff of the spinnaker will tend to collapse or, worse, it may not fly at all.

If your sail does collapse too quickly and feels very 'twitchy' to trim, have a look at the sail from off the boat and decide if the shoulders are too big. Look for the tell-tale creases from the head; these indicate that the shoulders are so big that they are pushing inwards, into the sail.

If the shoulders are too big, ask the sailmaker to re-fair the luffs. Removing a few inches from either luff will dramatically reduce the sails' tendency to collapse.

Sail too full

A very deep spinnaker may appear to fly well, but seems to suffer from a general lack of performance, especially when running.

Below: The foot panel on this spinnaker is fluttering on a tight reach.

Below: The spinnaker tapes are too tight, causing the luff to hook.

A spinnaker which is too full in the middle and head will not project as great an area as a flatter sail. The luff and leech will appear rounded and tight, and the shoulders will appear very small. The deeper the spinnaker, the harder it is for the stalled airflow to move off the sail. A pocket of stagnant air may develop in the deepest part of the sail and as a result, any flow across the sail is reduced.

The performance of a sail which is marginally too full can be improved by over-squaring the pole a little. The further apart you trim the leech and luff, the flatter the sail will fly. A spinnaker which is much too full will have to be completely re-cut, and all the broadseams will have to be reduced.

Hooked luff or leech

If the luff of the spinnaker appears hooked or curled the chances are that the luff tapes are too tight. The reason could be that the thread tension is too tight or poor-quality tapes have been used which shrink on wetting.

Below: This spinnaker is backwinding the main excessively. The barber hauler should be let off and the pole over-squared and lowered to encourage the clew to fly up and to leeward.

To rectify the problem the luff tapes have to be removed and resewn very carefully with a loose but even tension.

Foot panel flutters on close reach

Another common complaint with spinnakers is that the foot panel flaps noisily as the boat heads up onto a close reach. What happens is that the foot is stretched out tight, forming a crease between the two clews. Any cloth below that line which is unsupported and held in less tension will flap in the breeze.

To cure the problem, ask your sailmaker to increase the tension throughout the foot panel and put some shape into it by taking in a couple of vertical darts. Alternatively, the amount of unsupported foot round could be reduced, although this means losing some projected area when running downwind.

7 Care and repair

While modern sailcloth may appear very tough, it is a mistake to believe that sails do not need to be looked after. All sails, whether Dacron or Mylar, should be rinsed in fresh water after exposure to salt water or dirt. Any salt crystals left within the weave will chafe the adjacent fibres, causing premature cloth breakdown. The hygroscopic (water-attracting) salt crystals prevent the sails from drying off properly, causing corrosion of any metal fittings on the sail such as press rings (eyes) and headboard rivets.

FOLDING AND STORING

After washing and drying, yarn tempered sails should be carefully rolled from the head down. You can leave the battens in to help support the rolled sail and prevent it from being folded. As the resin dressing holds the fabric so stiffly, any tight creases tend to crack the finish and break the underlying fibres. Most creases occur while

Above: Mylar or yarn tempered sails should be rolled to prevent the formation of tight creases.

moving the sails around, so the best place to store them is inside a roll bag, laid out in the boat, under the cover. Mainsails made of softer cloth

Left and below: Soft sails made of a material such as Dacron should be loosely flaked concertina-style, then rolled into a loose bundle.

can be loosely flaked rather than rolled, as long as you use a different fold line each time. This method produces a lot of non-permanent creases which blow out easily.

Sailmakers will always tell you not to leave sails flogging on the boat, as this greatly accelerates cloth breakdown. Take your sails down while the boat is on the beach. Many sailors wrap their jibs around the forestay before launching or in between races. This practice is fine in light airs, but if you leave your jib furled on a windy day, you may come back after lunch to find the sail half unwound, flogging violently from side to side and the forestay chafing through the luff.

PREVENTING WEAR AND TEAR

To ensure that your brand new sails do not get ripped first time up, scour the boat for any sharp projections, and remove them or tape them up. The worst offenders are cotter pins, broken wire strands and projecting screw heads. Pay particular attention to the area around the spinnaker chute or bags, and make sure the spreader tips are well taped.

Spreader patches

You would be amazed at how may new sails come back to the sail loft for repair because the spreader has poked through the leech first time up, the owner having failed to fit the spreader patches supplied.

Spreader patches are only necessary on boats with large overlapping genoas, which can get pinned against the spreader when the sail is backed for too long. Sailmakers normally supply the self-adhesive Dacron patches loose with the sail, as

the correct position will vary from boat to boat depending on spreader height and mast rake. One-design boats which often require spreader patches include International 14s, Dragons and J24s.

To fit a patch, hoist the sail, mark where the spreader tip touches the leech and note the angle at which the patch should be set. Next, take the sail down and find a clean, flat surface where you can smooth the sail out flat. Working from the inboard end, peel a few inches of the backing paper off the patch and stick the end down in the chosen position. Check the patch is angled correctly; if not, there is still time to rip it off and try again. Then slowly peel the backing paper off towards the leech, pushing any air bubbles out from under the cloth as you go. At the leech cut the cloth flush. Then repeat the process for the other side of the sail, wrapping the last inch of cloth around the leech.

Jib luff protection

A common area of chafe on many dinghies is on the jib luff tape, where the spinnaker pole rubs against the luff wire and cuts through the cloth. One answer is to use plastic-coated wire, but it is then impossible to use a tension meter on the forestay.

The best solution is to get your sailmaker to fit a section of Teflon tape over the affected area, which is tough enough to cope with any amount of chafe.

Flutter patches

Leech 'flutter patches' have recently been allowed by the I.Y.R.U. and these help prolong the life of

Right: Teflon tape prevents the spinnaker pole chafing the jib luff.

Below: A flutter patch prevents the seam stretching at the leech, where the load is greatest.

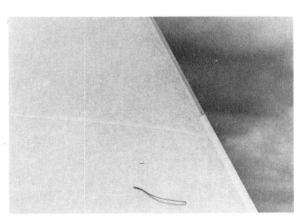

the leech. They consist of small, triangular Dacron patches sewn or stuck over the last few inches of the seams; they reduce the stretch at each seam and hence reduce the likelihood of the leech fluttering.

Battens

It is a sailmaker's nightmare to see battens flying out of his mainsail as the sail flogs before the start. At important regattas you should take no chances and sew the battens in with a quick stitch, or tape across the pocket.

Changing sail numbers

Removing numbers from a sail is not as easy as one might imagine. The cloth will peel off fairly easily, but the adhesive layer is invariably left firmly stuck to the sail. The only way to remove this sticky mess is to soak the area in acetone or carbon tetracholoride until the glue becomes loosened and can be scraped off. Be careful to place a plastic sheet underneath the sail when using the solvent, as stains and marks from the floor can wash through into the sail.

When the acetone has dried off, the new numbers can be applied. Check that the spacing between the numbers is in keeping with the class rules and that the number is located correctly on the sail. If there is no mention in the class rules,

then the I.Y.R.U. rule 25.1 applies: 'numbers shall be above an imaginary line projecting at right angles to the luff from a point one-third of the distance, measured from the tack, to the head of the sail; shall be clearly visible; and shall be placed at different heights on the two sides of the sail, those on the starboard side being uppermost.'

Some regatta sailors like their sail numbers placed as close as possible to the leech, so that their numbers are not so easily taken if they are caught over on the start line! In order to reduce the number of digits across the sail place the national letter on a separate line, above the numbers.

Running repairs

Damaged and torn sails are best repaired by the sail loft which built them. If a whole panel needs to be replaced it can be re-cut accurately from the original pattern, and the cloth can be matched exactly.

However, according to Sod's Law, you are

Below: Applying sail numbers and letters. (1) Smooth the sail out on a flat surface, and carefully position the number. (2-4) Begin to peel off the backing paper (starting at the top). Stick the top edge of the number to the sail then gradually peel off the paper, allowing the number to 'fall' onto the sail. If the shape is complex, cut the backing paper so you apply one half at a time.

1

3

2

4

most likely to rip a sail half-way through a regatta, when you have come ashore at 6 pm, the next race is at 10 am the following morning, and the local sailmaker has already left for the cheese and wine reception! The answer is to carry your own sail repair kit and learn how to deal with minor repairs yourself.

Ask the sailmaker for some off-cuts of your mainsail, jib and spinnaker cloth, suitable for patching. You may be able to buy a ready-made repair kit, and if possible it should include:

- Patch cloth for main, jib and spinnaker
- Self-adhesive insignia cloth and tape
- Spinnaker repair tape
- Spinnaker luff tape
- Webbing
- Hand-sewing needle and thread
- Pins

Spare hardware:

- Clew slug
- Batten end protector
- Spare battens
- Extra telltales
- Silicon spray
- Double-sided sticky tape for seams
- Press rings or grommets and tools

Small holes or chafe patches can be held together temporarily with self-adhesive insignia cloth; larger rips have to be cut out and replaced by a 'window patch', for which you will need a sewing machine.

Applying a window patch

1. Take the damaged area and pin it out flat on a smooth surface. Decide on the size of the patch, which should be kept clear of seams if possible. Ensure the direction of weave in the patch matches the sail (i.e. the warp and fill threads line up) and trim the patch to size.
2. Apply double-sided tape to the edges of the patch and stick it down flat. Unpin the sail and hold up the patched area to check there are no bumps.
3. Machine around the patch with two rows of zig-zag stitches.
4. Cut back the damaged cloth to the inside of the patch, and seal the cut edge with a hot knife.

Repairing spinnakers

The spinnaker is the sail which invariably receives most wear and tear. It used to be possible to repair the majority of spinnaker rips with self-adhesive spinnaker repair tape, but with the increasing use of highly resinated cloths this is no longer possible and tears have to be repaired by window patching.

When sewing a patch on a silicon-coated spinnaker, it may be necessary to hold the patch in place with dressmaking pins, if the double-sided tape is not sticking.

If the rip cuts right across one of the luff tapes, you will need to 're-fair' the luff. First patch the tear as before then pin the luff out flat to remove any wrinkles. It should now be possible to see the curved shape of the luff. Use a long sail batten to help re-draw the luff curve across the patched area. You may need to allow extra luff hollow to obtain a smooth and fair curve down the length of the luff.

1

Left and below: Repairing a hole. (1) Laying out the damaged sail. (2) Preparing the patch. (3) Sticking the patch over the hole. (4) Cutting back the damaged material.

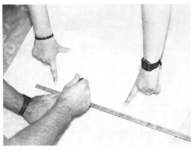

2

3

4

Other books in the Sail to Win series

Tactics   *Rodney Pattisson*
A guide to boat-to-boat tactics and strategy around an Olympic course, by gold medallist Rodney Pattisson.

Dinghy Helming   *Lawrie Smith*
One of Britain's top helmsmen gives specific advice on maximising boatspeed in all conditions, plus helming skills required during the race itself.

Dinghy Crewing   *Julian Brooke-Houghton*
Crewing a modern racing dinghy is a complex and demanding task. Olympic medallist Julian Brooke-Houghton explains the skills required and shows how helmsman and crew work together as a race-winning team.

Wind Strategy   *David Houghton*
Most 'sailing weather' books are too large-scale to be relevant to racing on inland or coastal waters. This book shows how to predict the wind over the racecourse area, during the time-span of the race, using simple 'rules of thumb'.

Tuning Your Dinghy   *Lawrie Smith*
A logical, systematic approach to setting up a racing dinghy and fine-tuning it on all points of sailing. Plus a 'trouble shooting' section to pinpoint and cure specific weaknesses in the boat's performance.

The Rules in Practice   *Bryan Willis*
It is a popular fallacy among racing sailors that you need to know the rules. You *do* need to know your rights and obligations on the water – the rules can always be looked up afterwards. International rules experts Bryan Willis looks at the key situations that repeatedly occur on championship courses, from the viewpoint of each helmsman in turn, and summarises what you may, must or cannot do.

Tides and Currents   *David Arnold*
How tides can help you win races – whether inshore, offshore or on an Olympic triangle.

Boatspeed – Supercharging your hull, foils and gear   *Rodney Pattisson*
Written by an Olympic Gold Medallist, this book gives the secrets of achieving a really fast boat – whether new or second-hand – plus detailed information on choosing and installing all the control systems.

The Winning Mind – Strategies for successful sailing   *John Whitmore*
Ninety per cent of sailing takes place from the neck up, yet most books concentrate on the hardware and on technique. *The Winning Mind* will not only help the sailor to perform better and more consistently but also help him and his crew enjoy their sailing to the full. Equally useful to the casual fair-weather sailor or the Olympic racer.

Also published by Fernhurst Books

Sailing the Mirror   *Roy Partridge*
Topper Sailing   *John Caig*
The Laser Book   *Tim Davison*
Laser Racing   *Ed Baird*
Yacht Crewing   *Malcolm McKeag*
Yacht Skipper   *Robin Aisher*
Boardsailing: a beginner's manual   *John Heath*
Board Racing   *Geoff Turner & Tim Davison*
Dee Caldwell's Book of Freestyle Boardsailing   *Dee Caldwell*
Must I go down to the sea again?   *Lesley Black/illustrated by Mike Peyton*
Knots & Splices   *Jeff Toghill*